ESTHER

SILENT BUT SOVEREIGN

10 Publishing
a division of 10 of those.com

First published in Great Britain in 2015

British Library Cataloguing in Publication Data

A record for this book is available from the British Library

ISBN: 9781909611849

Designed by Diane Bainbridge

Printed in the UK

10Publishing, a division of 10ofthose.com
9D Centurion Court, Farington, Leyland, PR25 3UQ, England
Email: info@10ofthose.com
Website: www.10ofthose.com

Esther

30 UNDATED DEVOTIONS THROUGH THE BOOK OF ESTHER

INTRODUCTION

'Where are you, God?' I'm sure most of us have at some time found ourselves in a situation that has challenged our faith and prompted that searching question.

The story of Esther is one of hope for those of us who find ourselves doubting God's sovereignty when we can't hear His voice or see what He is doing. We don't see God's name as we read through the pages of the story. He is not even mentioned at all. He is seemingly silent throughout the whole book, and yet He is actively working in every scene to bring about His purposes for His people.

It's my prayer that as you look into the book of Esther, you'll see and understand more of God's sovereignty, more of His faithfulness to His people, and more of His commitment to deliver and save. And that you'll be more equipped to trust Him even when it's not clear what He's doing.

The narrative of Esther is fast paced. For the sake of daily devotions that are manageable, we have broken up the readings into short passages. The down-side to this is that some of the original pace and drama can be lost. We therefore suggest that you read through the whole of Esther before you begin the devotions.

DAY 1

READ Esther 1:1–3

The story of Esther is set in Susa, the capital of the Persian Empire. Verse 1 tells us that the Persian Empire extended from India to Cush (Ethiopia), over 127 provinces. That made it the largest and most powerful empire in the world and King Xerxes, who ruled over the empire, the most powerful man in the world at that time.

Many years before Esther's story begins, the Jews experienced civil war and the Jewish nation was divided into two kingdoms. The Northern Kingdom was called Israel, and the Southern Kingdom, Judah. Most of the kings of Israel and Judah didn't walk with God consistently, so God judged them because of their unfaithfulness. First, Israel was attacked by Assyria and captured. Then, over 100 years later, Nebuchadnezzar invaded Judah, deported the King to Babylon and removed the temple treasures –we read about this in 2 Kings 24. Eleven years later Nebuchadnezzar returned, destroying Jerusalem and taking most of the Jews into captivity.

It could have seemed to the Jews, and to the surrounding nations, that God had finally deserted them. But although invisible He was active, ordering the events of history in such a way as to preserve His people and keep them from being completely destroyed by the Babylonians.

In 539 BC Babylon fell into the hands of the Medo-Persians and around 486 BC – 100 years after the fall of Jerusalem – Xerxes became king of the vast Persian Empire.

The book of Esther records a small piece of history, spanning ten years, of the life of the Jews living in exile in Persia. It may have seemed to the exiled Jews that God had completely turned His back on them and was no longer working to deliver and save them from their enemies. But as the story of Esther unfolds, we will see that God is always working for His people's good; He is never inactive.

Maybe you've experienced devastating blows in the past that you've not yet recovered from. Maybe fears about the future overwhelm you. Perhaps you're currently experiencing trials that threaten to pull you under a rising tide of despair and doubt. In the midst of such desperation, God is there. The book of Esther shows us that He doesn't stand by passively, watching His people suffer, but He is actively working to bring about their deliverance.

REFLECTION

What issues and cultural trends do we face in contemporary society that might cause us to doubt God's concern for His people? What truths about God's character can we call to mind in times of doubt or uncertainty?

DAY 2

READ Esther 1:4–9

Xerxes was in the third year of his reign, having defeated Egypt at war, when he gave a great banquet. Verse 4 tells us that the banquet lasted 180 days and was an extravagant exhibition of King Xerxes' greatness and wealth. This banquet was probably given as a reward to military officers and noblemen from all over the kingdom and was possibly also an opportunity to plan for the upcoming invasion of Greece.

At the end of the six-month-long banquet, King Xerxes gave another banquet that lasted seven days. This banquet was for everyone who lived in the citadel of Susa. No-one was excluded, from the greatest to the least. Again, it was a lavish banquet. Verse 7 records that: 'Wine was served in goblets of gold, each one different from the other, and the royal wine was abundant, in keeping with the king's liberality.' The guests could drink a little or a lot, or not at all if they chose. Everyone was free to do as they wished.

Verse 6 describes the garden of the king's palace in Susa and shows that life in the Persian Court during King Xerxes' reign was luxurious. They feasted on fine foods and drank from gold cups. The Persian court was dripping with wealth and extravagance.

King Xerxes was an incredibly powerful and proud king. At the beginning of his reign he was the most powerful man on earth. Archaeologists excavating at Susa have found inscriptions from that time in which King Xerxes refers to himself as, 'The great King, The King of Kings; The King of the lands occupied by many races; The King of this great earth.' He obviously thought a lot of himself and very little about the God of Israel.

In contrast, read Philippians 2:5–11. Compare Xerxes' pride with the humility of Jesus, the true 'King of kings'. In his pride, Xerxes believed that he was greater than God Himself. How do you view yourself? Does your attitude reflect the humility of Jesus or are you tempted to believe that you are more important than God and others?

True greatness is demonstrated in humble self-sacrifice. Jesus said,

'... whoever wants to become great among you must be your servant, and whoever wants to be first must be slave of all. For even the Son of Man did not come to be served, but to serve, and to give his life as a ransom for many' (Mk. 10:43–45).

REFLECTION

What does your lifestyle say about your priorities? Are you using every resource God has given you for His kingdom and glory or do you live for your own pleasure and satisfaction?

DAY 3

READ Esther 1:10–12

How do we respond when we're asked or pressured to behave in a way that opposes God's design for us?

Unsurprisingly, the seven-day garden party led to excess and inappropriate behaviour on the part of King Xerxes. He wanted to show off his beautiful wife, Queen Vashti, for all his drunken guests to enjoy (vv. 10–11). It's unclear whether the king was ordering Vashti to appear in *just* her royal crown and no other clothing or whether he wanted her to appear unveiled before his male guests to show off her beautiful face. To appear in court without her veil would have been scandalous in those times and Vashti would have suffered a loss of dignity and respect from the palace staff and royal officials who were all present. Either way it was a demeaning request for Xerxes to make of his wife, and Vashti courageously refused (v. 12).

Was Vashti right to disobey Xerxes? More importantly for us, in light of the New Testament commands for wives to be submissive to their husbands, are there circumstances in which it would be right for a Christian wife to disobey? The apostle Paul is clear in his letters that God's design for marriage is that husbands should love their wives 'as Christ loved the church and gave himself up for her' and that a wife is to submit to husband 'as ... to the Lord' (Eph. 5:22–25). But God's command for a wife to submit to her husband is not without limits; she submits to him 'as ... to the Lord'. He hasn't given a husband the right to fulfil any sinful or self-serving desire he might have through the unthinking obedience of his wife. He doesn't require a woman to lose the dignity she has as a human being made in the image of God by allowing her godly principles to be trampled underfoot by an ungodly husband. The authority that a man has is given to him by God. So when he disobeys or dishonours the Lord with that authority, there is a higher authority to which a woman must submit. She must obey and honour Jesus.

We can't assume that Queen Vashti was a godly woman; it's unlikely that she had a relationship with God. If she practised any sort of religion, it's likely that she was Zoroastrian. But despite not belonging to the people of God, Vashti's refusal to obey her husband's order was a dignified response to an undignified request. It demonstrated great bravery for her to oppose the powerful king in this way and verse 12 tells us that 'the king became furious and burned with anger'.

Xerxes wanted to flaunt his queen's beauty in the same way he flaunted his wealth and power. She was a trophy; an object to add value to his status. Modern attitudes towards women are often just as degrading and devaluing. But God's design for manhood and womanhood is both good and loving. He gives dignity to men and women and in Jesus both find equal worth and significance (Gal. 3:28).

REFLECTION

Pray that you will have a biblical understanding of manhood and womanhood that will result in behaviour and choices that are consistent with God's perfect design.

Think of a scenario in which obedience to God's Word may mean refusing to obey someone in a position of authority over you. Are you willing to face adverse consequences for the sake of being obedient to the Lord?

DAY 4

READ Esther 1:13–22

Queen Vashti's refusal to obey the king's order angered Xerxes and triggered a vengeful response. He sought counsel from his closest advisors, who are listed by name (v. 14) to distinguish them from the eunuchs who had been sent to bring Vashti before him earlier (v. 10).

These advisors are described in verse 13 as 'wise men who understood the times', but their advice on this occasion sprang from fear that they, along with all other men in the kingdom, were about to lose control of their wives and suffer disrespect and discord once news of Vashti's 'conduct' was made public.

The proposed solution was twofold: first, to demean Queen Vashti by banishing her from the king's presence and giving her position to someone 'better' (v. 19); second, to continue the domination of women throughout the empire by issuing a decree that would further diminish their role in society (v. 20).

Today this reads as a gross overreaction fuelled by pride and paranoia. The wealthiest, most powerful man on the earth, in a drunken moment, followed foolish advice and made a rash decision resulting in the dethronement and banishment of his beautiful queen. The decree that Vashti could never again enter the king's presence was made public throughout each province of the kingdom and irreversible by the law of the Medes and Persians.

But in the midst of all that was happening in the palace, God was working on behalf of His people. He was committed to His promise to preserve them and keep them from being wiped out. He had already prepared someone to fill the space made in the king's household by the banishment of Vashti.

King Xerxes had displayed his splendour, majesty and wealth for six months, but the Lord was the true ruler in Susa; silent but sovereign, He was working for His people's deliverance and salvation.

In 2008 tragedy struck the family of Christian singer Steven Curtis Chapman and his wife, Mary Beth, when one of their daughters was hit and killed by her older brother as she ran in front of the car he was driving. As she buried her five-year-old daughter, Mary Beth cried, 'God, where were you? Where are you?' A year later she wrote these words on her blog:

It might on certain days be buried deep down in my heart ... but here is what I know and what I choose to believe, over and over again. I know God loves me and my family. I know God is sovereign and He knows what is best for us. I know He has our days numbered and makes ***no*** *mistakes. I know that He will bring beauty from ashes ... that is what I cling to in order to make it through another twenty-four hours ... I have to* ***choose*** *to believe this right now.*[1]

It is often the case that we have to *choose* to see God in the midst of trials and difficulties. It is a choice to believe that He is sovereign. It is a choice to trust Him, even when we can't see what He is doing.

REFLECTION

Is there a situation in which you're struggling to believe that God could work for your good and His glory?

DAY 5

READ Esther 2:1–4

There are at least three years between the end of Esther chapter 1 and the beginning of chapter 2. Xerxes gave his banquet in the third year of his reign. We read in verse 16 that Esther was taken to him in the seventh year of his reign, having first completed twelve months of beauty treatments in accordance with the king's order (v. 12). In between this time, history records a disastrous attempt by King Xerxes to conquer Greece.

During this attack on Greece, Xerxes' mind may have been too focused on the battle to consider the consequences of Vashti's banishment. But as he returned to Susa, defeated and humiliated, perhaps he regretted his decision to banish Vashti and wished for the support and comfort of a wife. His attendants must have sensed King Xerxes' need for companionship, because they suggested a plan to find a replacement queen.

Like other monarchs of the time, King Xerxes would have had a harem full of women, and he certainly had the power to command any woman in the kingdom to appear before him whenever he wanted. So it seems that, in following the advice of his attendants, what he was looking for was not just a one-night stand or a casual relationship, but a replacement queen –a wife who would offer him intimacy and stability. Perhaps he also felt that a beautiful queen would improve his image following his defeat in battle.

As is the case in our culture, the Persians were obsessed with physical beauty, so the attendants' plan for a national beauty contest would ensure that the king's next wife would be the most beautiful woman in Persia. We're told later in verse 12 that this woman's beauty was enhanced with preparations and make-up for a whole year to make her presentable before the king. One commentator says that these words in verse 12 mean 'to rub, to polish, to purify and adorn with all kinds of precious ointments'.[2]

Most of us don't have the means or opportunity to pamper and enhance our appearance for twelve months, but we can often be influenced by our society's obsession with physical and temporary beauty more than by God's desire for us to cultivate beautiful hearts that reflect the character of Jesus. Perhaps at times we wish we were more beautiful, but Esther's exceptional beauty was given to her by God, not for her glory but to fulfil His purposes for His people.

REFLECTION

Read Colossians 3:12–14. Pray through the characteristics of a godly child of God. Which aspects do you need to cultivate more? Ask the Holy Spirit to work within you to make you more like Jesus in these areas of your life.

DAY 6

READ Esther 2:5–11

Verses 5–7 transfer our attention from the palace to the home of a man named Mordecai. We're told that Mordecai was a Jew from the tribe of Benjamin and that he was living in Susa.

It seems that Mordecai's great-grandfather was one of the Jews who had been taken into exile from Jerusalem by Nebuchadnezzar. Although some of the Jews had since returned to Jerusalem, Mordecai was still living in Persia, in the citadel of Susa, close to the king's palace.

Mordecai was raising his orphaned cousin, Hadassah, also known by her Persian name, Esther. Verse 7 tells us that Mordecai had taken Esther 'as his own daughter when her father and mother died'. This suggests that he was a man of integrity and compassion.

Even after Esther entered Xerxes' palace, we're given the lovely picture of a concerned and protective guardian, as we read that every day Mordecai 'walked to and fro near the courtyard of the harem to find out how Esther was and what was happening to her' (v. 11). He was not a man who had adopted his younger cousin out of a begrudging sense of duty, eager to be shot of his responsibility as soon as possible. Mordecai showed a continuing commitment to Esther and a deep concern for her well-being, even after she left his home for the palace. Mordecai's love towards Esther contrasts starkly with Xerxes' self-love.

We're also introduced in verses 5–7 to Esther, the orphan being raised by her older cousin, Mordecai. However loved and cared for she was by Mordecai and however much she loved him, Esther knew the devastation and crushing pain of losing not just one but both of her parents at a young age. She had experienced tragedy, but God was working so that years later Esther would be instrumental in saving the Jews.

The only other detail we read about Esther at this point is that she was very beautiful; verse 7 says she 'had a lovely figure and was beautiful'. She was an insignificant Jew and had no connection with powerful King Xerxes. But God, in His sovereignty, was weaving their lives together to accomplish His purposes for His people.

There are many examples in the Bible of people whose circumstances were sometimes tragic from a human perspective, but in God's sovereignty led to triumph. Consider Job, Joseph, Ruth, Daniel and Paul. The greatest example by far though is that of Jesus, whose rejection and suffering on the cross won forgiveness of sins and peace with God for all who trust in Him.

REFLECTION

Are you able to trust God's sovereignty in disappointment or disaster? Do you look for His hand in every situation?

It's thought that there could have been as many as 400 women involved in King Xerxes' quest to find the next queen. But Esther was the one who caught the attention of Hegai, the eunuch in charge of the women in the palace harem. Verse 9 tells us that Esther 'pleased him and won his favour'. Because of this he gave her preferential treatment, providing her with beauty treatments, special food and maids selected from the king's palace.

Although we know that Esther was very beautiful, it's unlikely that it was just her external beauty that made her stand out among the most beautiful women in the kingdom. It's likely that her character and behaviour also attracted Hegai's attention.

But more significantly, God had chosen Esther to be Xerxes' next queen and every detail of her journey from obscurity to royalty was ordained by Him. *He* caused Hegai to favour Esther and treat her with extra care. *He* would later move Xerxes' heart to choose her as his queen. God's sovereignty, faithfulness and power are seen in the events that led to Esther's coronation. His mercy, compassion and love are seen in the details of Esther's experience in the harem.

We're told in verse 8 that Esther was brought to the king's palace. We don't know whether this was by force, but we can assume some reluctance on her part, knowing that regardless of whether she was chosen to be queen, there was little chance of her returning home once she'd become part of the harem.

Esther was a young Jewess. She was protected and cared for by a guardian she loved and respected: Mordecai. It's unlikely that she would want to leave her loving home and the prospect of a Jewish marriage for life in a harem, no doubt filled with rivalry and jealousy and where she would be used for loveless sex for as long as she was considered to be beautiful.

The fact that Mordecai told Esther to keep her nationality a secret (v. 10) suggests there was potential danger for her as a Jew in the palace environment. So it's likely that she would have been frightened as she was taken to the harem. But God protected Esther and provided for her. He gave her grace and humility to endure her circumstances. He sustained her so that He could fulfil His purposes for His people. We often face situations in life that we wouldn't choose. Perhaps even now you're struggling with ill health or financial ruin; fighting with family members or friends; feeling rejected by a spouse, child or parents; or working in an ungodly environment. Do you struggle to see God's purposes in your situation?

Jesus understands how we feel in these times. Like Esther, He had to leave His home and experience loneliness and separation in order to fulfil God's purposes to save His people. Like Esther, He was surrounded by sinful behaviour and faced the temptation to compromise. But He submitted to His Father's will and even on the cross, His love, grace and forgiveness were evident (Lk. 23:34).

REFLECTION

Pray that in difficult circumstances you will be able to see God's compassion, mercy and love and trust in His faithfulness, power and sovereignty.

DAY 8

READ Esther 2:12–16

Esther was given special treatment by Hegai when she entered the king's harem. She was given her own maids, the best living quarters and special food. Her beauty treatments were started immediately (v. 9), so she would have been one of the first women to be ready to meet the king.

At least a year later, when each woman was ready to be presented to the king, verse 13 tells us that 'anything she wanted was given to her to take with her from the harem to the king's palace'. But Esther showed restraint and self-control, asking 'for nothing other than what Hegai ... suggested' (v. 15).

The point of the contest was to please the king and gain his favour, in order to be named the next queen. Most women would have taken advantage of every possible extravagance offered them so that they could make themselves as appealing as possible to win the king's favour. Esther displayed a modest restraint that reflected her trust in God for her future. She had no particular ambition to be crowned a queen.

Isaiah 30:15 says, 'in quietness and trust is your strength'. Israel didn't live out this promise and consequently ended up in captivity, but it seems that in the intimidating and godless palace of proud King Xerxes, Esther displayed a quiet trust in God and this was her strength.

The replacement queen was not judged by King Xerxes on her looks alone. We're told that when a young woman was summoned, she spent the night with the king (v. 14). As well as pleasing him with her beauty, she also had to satisfy him sexually. Part of Esther's preparation would have been to teach her how to successfully seduce King Xerxes, but the respect he shows Esther in the chapters that follow suggests Esther retained her dignity despite this. It *is* possible for godly people to maintain their dignity even in the most undignified of situations. It *is* possible to lift up grace even in the most humiliating and degrading of circumstances.

Helen Roseveare worked as a missionary doctor in the Congo during the 1960s. She was held as a prisoner for five months and raped by rebel soldiers during the country's civil war. She writes in *Give Me This Mountain*,

> *They were brutal and drunken. They cursed and swore, they struck and kicked, they used the butt-end of rifles and rubber truncheons. We were roughly taken, thrown in prisons, humiliated, threatened.*[3]

Helen was later able to thank God for trusting her with this suffering and to consider it a privilege to suffer for Jesus. Despite being treated in an undignified and humiliating way, she was able to maintain her dignity and honour Christ with her submissive response to that trial.

REFLECTION

Pray for 'the unfading beauty of a gentle and quiet spirit, which is of great worth in God's sight' (1 Pet. 3:4).

DAY 9

READ Esther 2:12–18

Once in the harem, it would have been easy for Esther to have been swept along with the frenzied competition to become queen. She could have become so busy rushing from one pampering session to the next that her ties with Mordecai could easily have become severed. It's a mark of her humility, respect and teachable spirit that Esther continued to follow Mordecai's advice even after leaving his home.

Esther had not told anyone her nationality because Mordecai had warned her not to (v.10). Having gained Hegai's favour, Esther could have become complacent about following this advice. She could easily have thought that her position in the harem was secure because of her beauty and winsomeness, but she continued to follow Mordecai's instructions and did so even after she had been made queen (v. 20).

Verses 9, 15 and 17 tell us that Esther pleased and won the favour of Hegai, King Xerxes and everyone who saw her. Esther's external beauty would have been enhanced by the twelve months of beauty treatments, but *all* of the women would have benefited from these treatments and *all* would therefore have appeared more beautiful than when they were first taken to the harem. Why did Esther especially stand out?

Despite her difficult circumstances, God worked in Esther's life to develop the characteristics of grace and humility that won the favour of everyone who saw her. '*Everyone*' implies even the women in the harem who were competing against her for the king's attention. Ultimately God made Esther so attractive to Xerxes that 'he set a royal crown on her head and made her queen' (v. 17). He demonstrated his delight in Esther by throwing a banquet in her honour, proclaiming a national holiday and distributing extravagant gifts (v. 18).

Esther is a beautiful example of grace, but she is not the most beautiful example of grace in the Bible. She points to Jesus, who embodied grace in all its beauty. John 1:14 says that Jesus came from the Father 'full of grace and truth'. Like Esther, Jesus experienced loneliness, broken-heartedness, humiliation and separation from His Father. But He was consistently characterised by grace, even towards his enemies. He was submissive to the will of His Father. He was humble and patient. He was compassionate and forgiving.

God has placed us in our individual circumstances, with our own set of challenges and pressures, but He has also given us His Spirit so we can reflect His grace in them. How can we develop the qualities of grace that will be evident to everyone who sees us, even our enemies? We need to trust God to control the circumstances around us and seek to develop the beauty and dignity that will draw attention to Him.

REFLECTION

Are you waiting until your circumstances change before you allow God to shine His grace through you? Pray that God would transform you in your circumstances, however humiliating or frightening they may be, so that His grace and power are seen in you.

DAY 10

READ Esther 2:19–23

The second gathering of the virgins (v. 19) suggests that the king's officials continued to gather beautiful girls for the harem. This is unsurprising. It's unlikely that King Xerxes would have embraced a restrained life of monogamy, releasing hundreds of beautiful women from his court, just because he had found his next queen in Esther. He quickly dismissed his previous queen, Vashti, because of her failure to comply with his irrational wishes, and he was predisposed towards hedonistic living. Why would that stop now, just because he had found his next queen? He was in party mode again, banqueting and holidaying with extravagance.

After Esther's coronation, Mordecai secured a job as a palace official at the king's gate (v. 19). In the ancient Middle East, the king's gate was the equivalent of our law courts, a place where important business was carried out. Perhaps Esther had used her influence as the new queen to secure that position for her cousin. Mordecai was now in the perfect place to uncover an assassination plot against Xerxes and report it to Esther so that she could warn the king (vv. 21–22).

Here we see God's hand at work in ensuring that Mordecai would be in just the right place, at just the right time, ready to uncover the conspiracy against the king. Years later this event would be significant in the saving of God's people, the Jews.

We're not told why Bigthana and Teresh became angry with Xerxes. Perhaps they liked Queen Vashti and didn't want to see her replaced. Perhaps it was because he chose to marry Esther, an outsider of the court, rather than a daughter of one of the seven noble families of the kingdom, as was customary. Perhaps they resented having being made eunuchs when everyone else was partying. It could have been over something very minor but we're not told why.

Mordecai could have chosen to ignore the conspiracy to assassinate the king. Xerxes was self-serving and unpredictable. Esther was living in the palace as his queen, still hiding her nationality. Mordecai could have wondered if he and Esther would be safer with King Xerxes out of the way. But he made the decision to warn Xerxes, showing grace when he had the opportunity.

Esther's grace and humility were also evident in the way she gave credit for uncovering the plot to Mordecai. She could have taken credit herself, further securing her favour with the king, but she credited Mordecai and his name was recorded in the official historical chronicles as the one who saved the king's life (v. 23). This was to be significant in the days to come. Mordecai received no immediate reward or recognition for saving the king, but God was invisibly working to accomplish His purposes.

REFLECTION

God is always active. Even in seemingly insignificant events, His hand is working to achieve His perfect plans.

DAY 11

READ Esther 3:1–6

There is a gap of around five years between the events at the end of chapter 2 and the start of chapter 3. It was therefore about five years after Esther's coronation as queen that King Xerxes honoured Haman and commanded all the officials at the king's gate to kneel down and pay honour to him (vv. 1–2).

The second commandment states that we should not bow down to or worship any God other than the Lord (Ex. 20:4–5). But in the same way that we show respect to royals or rulers today by bowing or curtseying, it wasn't considered a violation of this commandment for the Jews to bow to those in positions of authority as an expression of respect. Why, then, did Mordecai refuse to honour Haman in this way? (v. 2)

Verse 1 tells us that Haman was an Agagite. Earlier passages in the Old Testament tell us that the Agagites (a clan of the Amalekites) were long-standing enemies of the Jews. For example, back in Deuteronomy 25:17–19 God commanded the Israelites, through Moses, to destroy the Amalekites because they showed no fear of God and attacked the Israelites when they were vulnerable.

Later, in 1 Samuel 15, King Saul was told by God to kill all of the Amalekites, along with their animals. However, Saul disobeyed and spared King Agag's life, so Samuel 'put Agag to death before the LORD' (1 Sam. 15:33). Consequently, the Agagites hated the Jews and, as the story was passed down through history from one generation to the next, Haman would have inherited this grudge against the Jews.

Verse 4 suggests that Haman's hatred of the Jews was known by the palace officials, because they told him about Mordecai to see if his 'behaviour would be tolerated, for he had told them he was a Jew'. But Mordecai refused to honour an Amalekite, an enemy of the Lord. He was prepared to risk disobeying the king's order rather than compromise in this way. In contrast to King Saul, who *lost* his crown by refusing to *obey* God's commands concerning the Amalekites (1 Sam. 15:26–28), Mordecai refused to *ignore* God's commands and ultimately this would *win* him a crown.

The Bible is clear that obedience to Christ will result in persecution. Jesus himself tells us this in John 15:18–21. Are you prepared to risk rejection and punishment for the sake of Christ? In what situations do you face pressure to deny or disobey Jesus? Read 1 Peter 4:12–19 and Matthew 5:10–12. How do these verses encourage you to respond to such pressure?

REFLECTION

Pray for Christians who face persecution for their faith in Jesus on a daily basis.

(See barnabasfund.org for more details.)

DAY 12

READ Esther 3:3–15

We're told that at least a few days passed without Mordecai bowing to Haman (v. 4). But it appears that Mordecai did not make a scene in refusing to honour him. Haman himself didn't notice Mordecai's refusal to bow until it was pointed out to him by the officials at the gate. Mordecai, despite his insistence that Esther keep her nationality a secret, revealed that he was a Jew (v. 4) and this revelation led to a disturbing chain of events.

Haman's pride was so wounded once he heard of Mordecai, and his anger so fuelled (v. 5), that he planned retribution not just for Mordecai, or even Mordecai's family, but for every Jew living in the kingdom (v. 6). He planned the annihilation of every Jew in the empire (about 15 million people) and he manipulated the king to accomplish his evil plan (v. 8) by appealing to Xerxes' vanity and greed (v. 9). Notice he didn't tell the King that it was the Jews he was planning to get rid of.

So the date was set, twelve months later (v. 7), for the extermination of every Jew in the kingdom (v. 13). The edict that went out was written in the name of the king and sealed with his ring (v. 12) and could not be changed according to the law of the Medes and Persians.

The edict to destroy the Jews went out in the first month, the month of Nisan (v. 7). This was the time that the Jews celebrated the Passover and remembered God's faithfulness in bringing them out of Egypt. Having celebrated God's *past* deliverance, God's people would now be challenged to trust that He would deliver them in the *future*.

We read in verse 15: 'The king and Haman sat down to drink, but the city of Susa was bewildered.' However, God was not taken by surprise. He was not bewildered or ambivalent. He was not confused or helpless. Although in the text there is no mention of God's activity, He *was* working. He may have seemed silent, but He was not asleep. He was working things out according to His sovereign will.

Five hundred years later, at the time of the Passover, it must have seemed that God's plan had been defeated as Jesus died on the cross. As darkness covered the land and Jesus breathed His final breath, hopes that He was God's promised rescuer were shattered. But His resurrection three days later confirmed the completion of God's perfect plan of salvation and the fulfilment of His promises. Sinful men, however powerful, are not able to hinder God's work of saving for Himself the people He has chosen.

REFLECTION

How often do you reflect on God's past faithfulness in rescuing you and bringing you into His kingdom? Can you trust Him that He will continue to be faithful to you in the future?

DAY 13

READ Esther 4:1–8

When faced with distressing news, we may react in a variety of ways. One response is to lock ourselves away in private grief, paralysed by despair or fear. Another is to bury our heads in the sand, denying the reality of our situation. Alternatively, we can blow up in anger at our situation and those around us.

Mordecai was deeply grieved by the King's edict, but he was not paralysed by his grief. '... he tore his clothes, put on sackcloth and ashes [the outward sign of mourning], and went out into the city, wailing loudly and bitterly' (v. 1).

Mordecai didn't stay home and grieve privately. He didn't hide away in case anyone found out he had been the reason for this edict. But neither did he wander around aimlessly. He went to the king's gate (v. 2). He couldn't enter the gate because of his sackcloth (it was considered impolite to express sadness in the king's presence), but nevertheless he went *to* the king's gate. Why? Because he wanted to communicate with Esther. Because he believed that God could use her to deliver His people. Because he believed that, in His providence, God had ordained the crowning of Esther for this very reason.

Mordecai didn't end up at the king's gate by chance. When Hathak went out to Mordecai to find out what was troubling him (vv. 5 6), 'Mordecai told him everything that had happened to him, including the exact amount of money Haman had promised to pay into the royal treasury' (v. 7). He must have done some research to find this out. He had also taken with him a copy of the text of the edict to pass on to Esther. His intent was to persuade Esther to approach the king and intercede for the Jews (v. 8).

It might seem surprising that Mordecai would choose to go to the public place where he was known to be Jewish. It would also have been known at the king's gate that his refusal to bow to Haman instigated the planned genocide of the Jews across Persia. He risked both mockery from his enemies and accusation from his fellow Jews as he made his way to the city square. But Mordecai was not preoccupied with his own fate; he was prepared to act on behalf of all of God's people.

Verse 3 communicates the bewildered and desperate response of Jews all over the kingdom of Persia as they received news of their impending destruction. But despite the devastating news of an imminent holocaust, Mordecai's faith in his faithful God spurred him into thoughtful activity.

In times of distress we can trust completely in God's unchanging love for us and His great power to work for us. We also need to be wise and thoughtful so that our outward behaviour is evidence of our inward faith.

REFLECTION

Pray Psalm 62 for yourself.

DAY 14

READ Esther 4:9–17

Esther was rightly frightened by Mordecai's instruction to go into the king's presence and plead with him for the Jews. No-one was allowed to approach the king in his inner court without an invitation. Xerxes was not immune from assassination attempts (Esth. 2:21), so this was partly to protect his life. He would extend his gold sceptre only to those he knew and welcomed a visit from. Anyone else entering his presence without being summoned was put to death (v. 11). Esther hadn't been called into the king's presence for thirty days (v. 11), so she was not confident that she would be received favourably by Xerxes.

But Mordecai's words in verses 13–14 encouraged her to exhibit faith without fear. He reminded Esther of God's sovereignty and faithfulness. He had promised to deliver His people and He could be trusted to do that. Mordecai also challenged Esther to recognise God's sovereignty in placing her in the unique position she was now in: as queen with the ear of the king.

When Esther sent Mordecai her second reply in verse 16, her words revealed her faith. After considering Mordecai's words, Esther was prepared to speak on behalf of the Jews, regardless of the consequences to her personally. Her hesitation was replaced by confidence and determination. Her fear gave way to faith and courage. Her concern shifted from that of her own safety to the survival of God's people. Ultimately, Esther demonstrated an eternal perspective: 'if I perish, I perish'. She wasn't afraid to die for her faith.

It's perhaps unlikely that we will die for our faith, but it may be that our reputations will suffer as we speak up for Jesus. It *is* likely that we will lose popularity and friends, maybe opportunities for job promotions, even the love and respect of family members as we demonstrate a courageous commitment to be God's mouthpiece in our society. But an eternal perspective shifts our focus from these temporary discomforts to the reward that is assured to those who are faithful.

The deliverance of the Jews wasn't Esther's responsibility – that was God's job. But Esther did have a responsibility to be faithful, obedient and available to be used by God in the situation He had placed her in.

Only Esther was in a position to approach King Xerxes and speak on behalf of the Jews as they faced an unjust death sentence. She alone could intercede for them, because she alone was both Persian royalty and a Jew. We have a far greater mediator. Only Jesus could intercede on our behalf to God the Father to save us from the just death sentence we faced because of our sin. He alone could sacrifice His life to save us because He alone was fully God and fully man.

REFLECTION

How is God calling you to be faithful and obedient in your current circumstances? Are you available to be used by Him?

'... who knows but that you have come to your royal position for such a time as this?' (v. 14). Mordecai wasn't content to let Esther live a quiet, complacent life in the palace. He wanted her to make a difference. He believed that God had equipped Esther with everything she needed to impact the situation the Jews were in and he challenged her to follow his example of courageous leadership.

If you're a parent, do you desire this same level of commitment from your children? Do you want your child to impact their situations for Jesus regardless of what it might cost them in terms of respect, popularity or academic achievement?

Are you encouraging younger Christians that you know to make a difference? How are you teaching them to stand up for Jesus and desire His honour above their own reputations?

Mordecai's faith in God encouraged him to expect great things of Esther. Our faith should encourage us to expect Him to do great things through us and through those we disciple. We should pray for godly strength and a courageous spirit both for ourselves and other Christians.

Think about your own places of influence and the people you regularly spend time with: your family; your friends; your work; church; your community; your gym; the school gate; the bus or train you catch regularly; your dentist, doctor, hairdresser, postman ... Where has God placed *you* so that *you* can make a difference? Are you ready to speak and act? God doesn't need us to accomplish His purposes. There are other people He could use. His plans won't be frustrated because we won't speak or act. But if we don't, we may miss out on the privilege and blessing of being involved in His work.

In his book *Don't Waste Your Life*, John Piper writes,

You don't have to know a lot of things for your life to make a lasting difference in the world. But you do have to know the few great things that matter, perhaps just one, and then be willing to live for them and die for them. The people that make a durable difference in the world are not the people who have mastered many things, but who have been mastered by one great thing.[4]

The apostle Paul had been 'mastered' by the gospel of Jesus. He wrote to the church in Philippi, 'For to me, to live is Christ and to die is gain' (Phil. 1:21). Paul lived to serve Jesus and His kingdom; nothing else mattered to him.

REFLECTION

Is the gospel of Jesus the 'one great thing' that has mastered you? Do you believe that you have been placed by God in every situation you're now in 'for such a time as this'?

DAY 16

READ Esther 4:15 – 5:8

When faced with a crisis, is our first response action or prayer? It's not easy to wait patiently on the Lord in prayer. To allow time for Him to work in our hearts to comfort, strengthen and renew perspective requires discipline. But as we spend time with God in prayer, He works, not only in our hearts but also in the circumstances and hearts of those around us.

As Esther, her attendants and the Jews waited on the Lord (4:16), God prepared Xerxes' heart so that he was prepared to meet any request she would make. Esther was not only allowed uninvited into his presence (5:1–2), but Xerxes consented to her request 'Even up to half the kingdom' (5:3). This was a fairly common phrase, used for show by proud, powerful men, wanting to impress. Xerxes didn't literally mean that he would hand half his kingdom over to Esther, but he was prepared to grant any reasonable request of hers because she found favour with him.

Esther had put on her royal robes, dressing respectfully for the king so that when he saw her 'he was pleased with her'. She didn't run foolishly into his presence, crying hysterically and pleading with him for mercy. She stood, poised and dignified, and waited until he called her to him.

While praying and fasting, Esther had also been preparing a feast that her husband would enjoy (5:4) – that must have taken some self-control! We know that Xerxes loved feasts so it was unsurprising that he would accept Esther's invitation. What *was* surprising was Esther's second choice of honoured dinner guest: the hated enemy of the Jews, Haman!

Esther didn't rush to point the finger at Haman, accusing him of his evil before the king and his court. Rather, she used Haman's pride and ambition to lure him into a false sense of security before, in God's time, exposing him before the king as her greatest threat, her potential murderer.

We don't know why God's timing required another day but, when prompted again by Xerxes to present her request (5:6), Esther continued to be patient, inviting Xerxes and Haman to dine with her the next day when she would answer his question (5:8).

Although apparently silent, it's clear that during the three days of prayer and fasting God was working. He was working in Esther to make her patient, wise, courageous and sensitive to His leading. God was also working in Xerxes' heart so that he was prepared to receive Esther and grant her requests. In our times of crisis, we too can be confident that our sovereign God is always working, even when He appears to be silent.

REFLECTION

Are you facing a situation that requires you to wait patiently on the Lord in prayer and trust that He will work for your good and His glory?

DAY 17

READ Esther 5:9–14

Unsurprisingly, Haman left the banquet in high spirits (v. 9). He'd dealt with the Jews; he'd enjoyed a private banquet with the king and queen; and he had another feast scheduled for the next day. Life was great!

Then he passed Mordecai, back in his position of work at the king's gate. Mordecai still refused to be impressed by Haman. He still refused to show respect and, perhaps surprisingly, he didn't show any fear either. Haman was provoked to rage (v. 9). But in his eagerness to get home, Haman restrained himself (v. 10).

It's interesting that Mordecai was back at work. Perhaps after three days of prayer and fasting, he trusted that God was working, so he decided to leave the problem of Haman's edict to God and get back to his responsibilities. He wasn't trying to interfere. He wasn't manipulating people or situations. He was just getting on with his work, minding his own business and leaving God to mind His.

But Haman was dissatisfied. He was completely unable to mind, or even enjoy, *his* own business. After boasting to his wife and friends about his elevated status, favour at the palace, wealth and number of sons (vv. 11–12), Haman expressed his dissatisfaction and resentment that Mordecai would still not honour him (v. 13).

Verse 14 records another instance of bad advice, this time given to Haman by his wife and friends:

Have a pole set up, reaching to a height of fifty cubits [about 23 metres], and ask the king in the morning to have Mordecai impaled on it. Then go with the king to the banquet and enjoy yourself.

In Persian times hanging was a shameful and tortuous way to die. Rather than being hung with a rope, victims were impaled on a sharpened wooden pole. It was an early form of crucifixion. Mordecai's wife, Zeresh, was suggesting an incredibly vicious and publicly humiliating death for Mordecai.

Haman's earlier plan had already ensured that Mordecai was scheduled to be killed in eleven months' time. But his rage had escalated to such a degree that he couldn't wait; only the immediate and agonising death of his enemy would satisfy him.

Five hundred years later Jesus Christ suffered a vicious and humiliating death at the hands of His enemies. Although deserving of honour and worship, He humbled Himself and experienced the righteous wrath of a holy God against sin. In contrast to Haman, who demanded reverence and respect that he was not worthy of, Jesus invites us to bow before Him in love. In contrast to Haman, who was full of hatred and vengeance fuelled by a centuries-old grudge, Jesus freely offers forgiveness and grace to anyone, regardless of our past offences against Him.

REFLECTION

Reflect on Jesus' humility and the mercy He has shown towards you. Thank Him for His sacrifice and pray for a gracious and humble spirit.

READ Esther 6:1–11

'In the LORD's hand the king's heart is a stream of water that he channels towards all who please him' (Prov. 21:1).

The night before Esther was to make her request, King Xerxes couldn't sleep. Instead of asking for food, wine, entertainment or even for a woman from his harem, he asked for the record of his reign to be brought in and read to him (v. 1) – perhaps he thought the historical account would send him to sleep!

Part of the history read to Xerxes was the account of the assassination plot by Bigthana and Teresh that Mordecai had saved him from (v. 2). Suddenly the king was wide awake! God had the king's heart in his hands, and at just the right time He prompted Xerxes to notice and honour Mordecai (v. 3).

On hearing that nothing had been done to honour the man who had saved his life five years earlier, Xerxes needed help in planning and carrying out an appropriate reward. Haman had just entered the court, having rushed to the palace at the crack of dawn desperate to petition the king about hanging Mordecai on the pole he'd had built (v. 4). So the king called him in; who better to help him formulate and execute his plan than his best friend and wise advisor, Haman?

In his pride Haman assumed that the person the king would most like to honour would be him, so he listed every honour he could imagine for himself (vv. 6–9). Imagine his humiliation when King Xerxes instructed him to bestow this list of honours upon his hated enemy, Mordecai (v. 10)! Imagine his rage and disbelief that his enemy, the one he'd planned to have killed that morning, would receive the honour that he thought was due to him! That Haman himself had to publicly bestow this honour on the king's behalf (v. 11) would have been doubly mortifying!

Haman illustrates the depravity of the human heart. It's easy to stand in judgement over him but we need to understand that without God's mercy we would be just like him. His pride dominates the middle chapters of the book of Esther. He craved public honour and recognition. He was desperate to wear the king's robes and crown. He was unforgiving and unrelenting in his pursuit of privilege and respect. He became increasingly proud, emulating the king he served, Xerxes.

The King we serve and are called to emulate is the complete opposite. Jesus stripped himself of honour and recognition. He gave up His royal robes and crown and instead wore a crown of thorns. He is full of forgiveness and unrelenting in His pursuit of lost people who need a saviour.

REFLECTION

In what ways are you more like Haman than Jesus? How does pride impact your gospel ministries?

DAY 19

READ Esther 6:11–14

Hebrews 6:10 tells us that, 'God is not unjust; he will not forget your work and the love you have shown him as you have helped his people and continue to help them.'

Mordecai never sought reward or recognition. He had continued to serve quietly and faithfully. But God, who had seen his faithfulness, stepped in to honour him. We don't read that Mordecai was pumping his fists in the air or encouraging chants or applause. We don't read that he was taunting Haman as he led his horse through the city. The only thing we read is that, 'Afterwards Mordecai returned to the king's gate' (v. 12).

He went back to work. He went back to minding his own business. He didn't take the day to rejoice in his changed fortune. Unlike Haman (see 5:10–12), he didn't rush home to boast and celebrate with his friends. He retained his humility and went back to work and back to waiting for God's next move.

Mordecai's example of humility is both refreshing and challenging. We so often strive for recognition, respect and privileges. Our hearts more often reflect Haman's attitude rather than Mordecai's. Humility is a rare but beautiful characteristic, and although the truly humble person never seeks man's approval or praise, their humility actually attracts others to them.

In his book *Humility: True Greatness*, C.J. Mahaney says that 'humility draws the gaze of God'.[5] We see that in Mordecai's life, but we also find that we ourselves are drawn to him because of his humility. Humility also draws the gaze of others.

Both Mordecai's and Esther's stories show the beauty of true humility and how it shines brightly against a backdrop of pride and greed. We see that beauty even more clearly when we consider the greatest example of humility, Jesus.

Read Philippians 2:5–11. Jesus is our ultimate example of true humility and grace. Although worthy of all honour and praise, He left the splendour of heaven's throne room and lowered Himself to become a man, not to be recognised as a great human king but as a servant; not to enjoy accolades and applause for His power and majesty but to endure a painful death on behalf of those He was seeking to save. The one who *was* God became nothing so that we, who deserve nothing but judgement for our pride and sin, could become righteous and receive royal crowns.

REFLECTION

Are you striving to be genuinely humble? In what areas of life is this especially challenging? Pray about these areas now.

DAY 20

READ Esther 6:1–14

In his book *Disappointment with God*, Philip Yancey writes:

No matter how we try to rationalize, God will sometimes seem unfair from the perspective of a person trapped in time. Only at the end of time, after we have attained God's level of viewing, after every evil has been punished, every illness healed, and the entire universe restored, only then will fairness reign. Then we will understand what role is played by evil, by the fall, and by natural law, in an 'unfair' event like the death of a child. Until then, we will not know, and can only trust in a God who does know ... Not until history has run its course, will we understand how 'all things worked together for good'. Faith then means believing in advance what will only make sense in reverse.[6]

Mordecai saved King Xerxes from an assassination plot against him. But he received no thanks or reward for this. Instead, King Xerxes honoured Haman the Agagite (3:1) and Mordecai continued to work at the king's gate.

Then Mordecai became the object of Haman's wrath and hatred because he wouldn't dishonour the Lord by bowing to Haman. When Haman planned to kill all of God's people, Mordecai had faith that God would deliver His people and he influenced Esther to speak on their behalf. Even Haman's wife and advisors later realised that if God was on Mordecai's side, Haman could not 'stand against him' and would 'come to ruin' (v. 13).

But despite Mordecai's integrity and faith, he faced a cruel and unjust execution.

It must have been difficult for Mordecai to understand what God was doing during those testing times. He believed in God's promises and faithfulness to His people, but he must have struggled to see how God was working for his good in his life.

The events recorded in Esther 6 show us that God hadn't forgotten Mordecai. He hadn't overlooked him as Xerxes had done. He was working, even through the night, to save Mordecai and honour him for his faithfulness.

Joni Eareckson Tada became a quadriplegic at age seventeen as a result of a diving accident. After the accident, she struggled to understand why God had allowed this tragedy in her life, but eventually she began to see her circumstances from a different perspective. She later said, 'Sometimes God allows what He hates to accomplish what He loves.'

Read Romans 8:28. Joni has said,

Most of the time we scratched our heads and wondered how the matted mesh of threads in Romans 8:28 could possibly be woven together for our good. On earth, the underside of the tapestry was tangled and unclear; but in heaven, we will stand amazed to see the topside of the tapestry and how God beautifully embroidered each circumstance into a pattern for our good and His glory.[7]

REFLECTION

How does Esther 6 encourage you to trust that God is always working for your good and His glory?

DAY 21

READ Esther 7:1–10

At the second banquet (v. 1) Esther was ready to reveal her request to the king. When asked by Xerxes what it was she wanted (v. 2), Esther replied graciously, showing respect for her husband and the important matters he was involved in (vv. 3–4). Xerxes was outraged that someone should plan to harm Esther and was ready to deal with the culprit (v. 5). Although Xerxes hadn't seen Esther for a month, in two days she had secured his favour again, not with deceitful or manipulative behaviour but with grace and dignity.

Esther had prayed and fasted. She had chosen her moment carefully, prompted by God. She was truthful. She didn't exaggerate the plight of the Jews. She didn't withhold the fact that she herself was a Jew and in danger. She was gracious and respectful. She was wise and patient. She was God's mouthpiece as she spoke up for His people.

Xerxes knew that Esther was telling the truth because her character was evident to him. Even when Esther revealed that the man who had plotted such a great atrocity was his most trusted friend, Haman (v. 6), Xerxes knew that what Esther said was true.

There is great humour in the next scene! King Xerxes stormed out of the room in a rage against Haman (v. 7). Haman, horror-stricken at the revelation that Queen Esther was one of the Jews he had planned to destroy, knew that his fate was decided and appealed to the queen to have mercy and intercede for him. In his desperate state, he inadvertently fell on to her just as Xerxes re-entered the room (v. 8)!

Of course Haman did not intend to molest the queen. But as soon as the exclamation of outrage left Xerxes' lips, the death sentence was pronounced and Haman's head was covered (v. 8), symbolising his demise. When Harbona, one of the king's eunuchs, informed him of the twenty-three metres-high pole that Haman had made at his house, ready to impale Mordecai on, the suggestion was obvious: 'Impale *him* on it!' (v. 9, my italics). So, in an ironic twist, Haman was impaled on the pole that he had prepared for Mordecai (v. 10)!

But this isn't just irony; it's God's surprising sovereignty! Although His name is not written in the pages of this book, His sovereign activity is stamped across it and it is God, not Esther, who is the focus of the story. His perfect, remarkable timing leaves us in no doubt that He is the one who is in charge. He is the one who controls all things, even the seemingly insignificant details of history. He is 'silent but sovereign'.

REFLECTION

How does this chapter encourage you to believe that God is always working for your good, even when you can't understand what He is doing?

DAY 22

READ Esther 8:1–10

In Persian times the property of condemned criminals reverted back to the crown. So it would be assumed that, after his execution, Haman's estate would become the property of Xerxes, the king who loved wealth and power. But we read instead that Xerxes gave Haman's estate to Esther (v. 1). He then gave his signet ring - his power to make decrees and edicts - to Mordecai (v. 2), who he'd only heard of early that morning. God had been working to soften the heart of this proud king.

Perhaps there is someone in your life who seems to have a hard and impenetrable heart. Perhaps there is someone who hates you or tries to humiliate you. Perhaps there is someone who intimidates or frightens you. There is no heart so hard that the Lord cannot soften it. We see that here in Xerxes' uncharacteristic kindness towards Esther and Mordecai. We have no reason to doubt God's power to change even the hardest heart today.

There is a gap of a couple of months between verses 2 and 3, when Esther once more petitioned Xerxes. Verse 9 tells us that Esther pleaded with the king again during the third month; Haman's first edict had gone out during the first month. Xerxes' heart had been softened, but although Haman was dead, his edict was still alive. It couldn't be revoked, according to the law of the Medes and Persians, so in nine months' time the Jews were to be slaughtered.

It is likely that Esther was fairly safe. She was a queen highly favoured by King Xerxes and it is unlikely that she would have been killed along with the Jews. Her words in verse 6 suggest she believed this herself: 'how can I bear to see disaster fall on my people? How can I bear to see the destruction of my family?' Esther's distress as she approached the king again was not for herself but for God's people, the Jews.

This time when Esther pleaded to the king on behalf of her people she was very emotional. She fell at his feet weeping, begging him to put an end to Haman's plan (v. 3). This wasn't a calculated performance, intended to manipulate her husband into doing what she wanted. She wept genuine, compassionate tears out of a heart that was heavily burdened for God's people.

Esther had a deep love for God's people, even those she didn't know. That presents a challenge for us. Do you love all of God's people, even those you don't know? God is passionate for His people. He loves us deeply, sacrificially, unconditionally. His Spirit in us means that we will be passionate for His people too. We will love each other deeply, sacrificially, unconditionally.

REFLECTION

How do you demonstrate love for God's people? In what practical ways do you demonstrate commitment to your church family?

READ Esther 8:7–14

'... weeping may stay for the night, but rejoicing comes in the morning' (Ps. 30:5).

Haman's law could not be reversed. But God moved King Xerxes' heart so that he allowed Esther and Mordecai to write another law that would offer the Jews protection from its effects.

Mordecai's law granted the Jews in every city in the kingdom the right to assemble and protect themselves on the thirteenth day of the twelfth month; the day that was scheduled for their destruction (v. 12). The edict permitted them to destroy and kill any armed force of any nationality that might attack them and also allowed them to 'plunder the property of their enemies' (v. 11). This command was taken to the Jews in every province by mounted couriers who rode especially fast horses. We're told they went out 'spurred on by the king's command' (v. 14).

Why was the edict delivered so quickly? For two months the Jews had been living with the threat of impending destruction weighing heavily on their hearts. The speed with which the edict was communicated is proof that Xerxes' heart had been softened. He was eager to let them know immediately of their salvation. The same king that had hastily signed an edict permitting genocide against the Jews was swift to provide a way of escape for them.

Unlike Haman's law, this wasn't a cruel and vengeful edict. Mordecai wasn't permitting murder inspired by hatred but rather self-defence in the face of attack. And this self-defence was only permitted on the day that the Jews were likely to be attacked by their enemies: the thirteenth day of the twelfth month. It's likely that once this edict was made public, along with news of Haman's hanging, at least some enemies of the Jews would have been less inclined to proceed with their own planned attacks.

Xerxes hadn't been able to reverse Haman's law, but he provided a way to prevent it from being effective. He allowed the Jews to protect themselves against attack and even kill anyone who might attack them. He also gave them nine months in which to prepare their defence.

Augustine said, 'God judged it better to bring good out of evil than not to permit any evil to exist.'[8] The Jews may have questioned why God allowed them to experience such overwhelming fear and despair for two months, if His purpose was always to spare them from destruction. We may question why God allows us to face desperation and grief that seems unnecessarily painful or cruel. We need to learn to trust that He has purposes that can only be accomplished through our experiences of suffering. We need to believe that our temporary troubles result in glory that far outweighs them all (2 Cor. 4:17).

REFLECTION

Read 2 Corinthians 4:7–18. What benefits does Paul say result from the Christian's suffering?

DAY 24

READ Esther 8:15–17

In these verses the humble, godly leadership of Mordecai stands in stark contrast with the proud, ungodly leadership we saw earlier in Haman.

Mordecai had been given the king's signet ring two months earlier. He had been working closely with the king since the demise of Haman. But it was only after he had secured salvation for the Jews that he left the palace wearing his royal robes and crown (v. 15). It was as if he could only be comfortable in his new, exalted position once he knew that his people were safe. Like Esther, Mordecai's humility remained intact despite his elevated status.

Haman had revelled in his high position and used it to accomplish his own vengeful purposes. He had been given the king's signet ring – the power to make decisions on his behalf. But he used that power to issue a death sentence against the people of God. He was dispassionate and merciless. His subsequent plan to kill Mordecai immediately on the pole he had built was born purely out of pride and malice.

In contrast, Mordecai used his influence with the king for the good of God's people. He wasn't content to enjoy comfort and wealth while his fellow Jews remained under the threat of death. He used the power of the king's signet ring to reverse Haman's death sentence. He was compassionate and full of mercy. His actions were motivated by a desire to protect and honour the Jews.

Haman's leadership had brought fear and desperation to the Jews living in Persia. Mordecai's leadership brought peace and rejoicing. Once Mordecai's edict was made known, the city of Susa held a joyous celebration. Verse 16 tells us: 'For the Jews it was a time of happiness and joy, gladness and honour.'

In the two months of Mordecai's influence at the palace, the fate of the Jews had been completely reversed. God had placed both Esther and Mordecai in positions of influence so that His people would be delivered. In addition to that, verse 17 records that 'many people of other nationalities became Jews because fear of the Jews had seized them'. God's mercy wasn't limited to the Jews; He used the reversal of Haman's edict to attract people from other nations to Himself.

Mordecai was a strong, godly leader. His priority was the honour of God's name and the deliverance of God's people. His motives were unselfish: he used his position to achieve God's glory in delivering His people rather than his own exaltation. His attitude was humble: he shared in the sufferings of the Jews and identified with them in their distress. He trusted in God's character: he believed that God was faithful and powerful to fulfil his promises to His people.

REFLECTION

Consider the challenges that face church leaders today. Pray for strong, godly, faith-filled leaders who are passionate about God's kingdom and willing to sacrifice for His glory.

Consider where you might be in a position of influence, with either believers or unbelievers. How can you demonstrate a humble, godly attitude that is motivated by a desire to honour God's people?

DAY 25

READ Esther 9:1–17

Mordecai's edict brought about a complete reversal of Haman's one. Verse 1 says,

On this day the enemies of the Jews had hoped to overpower them, but now the tables were turned and the Jews got the upper hand over those who hated them.

What a great summary of the whole book of Esther!

When the Jews assembled in their cities to defend themselves against their attackers, no-one could stand against them. Everyone was afraid of them (v. 2). They struck down their enemies and destroyed them. They killed 500 men in the citadel of Susa (v. 6) and also Haman's ten sons (v. 7). In the rest of the province they killed 75,000 of their enemies (v. 16).

The Jews weren't initiating the attacks; they were only permitted to defend themselves against those attacking them. We know they adhered to this principle because verse 3 tells us they were helped by all the important citizens of the province and the king's own administrators. Mordecai's edict deterred many men from sinning against God's people by attempting to kill them. Seventy-five thousand was a small percentage of the total number of Gentile men living throughout the province; most refrained from attacking the Jews.

Xerxes' response to the victory of the Jews in Susa was surprising. We might expect that he would be angry at the Jews or regretful of his decision to allow their defence. But he wanted Esther to be satisfied that justice was served and was prepared to grant a further request (v. 12).

Why did Esther request that the Jews in Susa be granted another day in which to attack their enemies and for Haman's sons to be hanged on the poles when they were already dead (v. 13)? Three hundred more men die (v. 15) but it's unlikely Esther was acting out of a vengeful desire to cause more pain to the non-Jewish citizens of Susa. It's more likely that she wanted to be sure that the threat to God's people really was eliminated. It's possible she believed the impaling of Haman's sons would serve as a public warning that God's people would not face that kind of threat again.

Everything that had been true for the Jews in Persia a year earlier was reversed. They were no longer frightened but victorious. They were no longer characterised by desperation but by rejoicing. They no longer feared death but embraced life.

As Christians everything that was true for us before our conversion has also been reversed. We no longer fear death because Jesus has been victorious over it. We are no longer desperate because of our sin but rejoice that Jesus' death and resurrection has dealt with it completely. We no longer face destruction but eternal life.

REFLECTION

Reflect on the changes that God has brought about in your life. How often do you thank Him for His work? Do you trust that He can reverse any situation that you're in?

DAY 26

READ Esther 9:1–17

The Jews in Persia had been living under the threat of death since Haman's edict was announced. Suddenly they were given permission not just to defend but to avenge themselves on their enemies. They were given an opportunity to retaliate to the terror they had been living with since Haman's edict was declared. They now had the opportunity to inflict terror on the Gentiles who had been planning to attack them and to benefit materially from their enemies defeat.

But we read three times in Esther 9 (vv. 10, 15, 16) that despite winning a great victory over their enemies, the Jews took no plunder. They'd been given freedom to take plunder from their attackers (8:11). They were entitled to take their property but they didn't. They defended themselves, but went no further than that.

The Jews had also been given permission to kill the wives and children of their attackers (ESV), but verse 12 says they 'killed and destroyed five hundred men and the ten sons of Haman in the citadel of Susa'. There is no record that they unnecessarily killed women and children, in that city at least.

In her book *Daylight at Midnight*, Jane McNabb suggests that this must have been a community decision because there were no exceptions throughout the entire empire. She says that the Jews' purity in this was a natural response to their own deliverance. Jane writes,

On the day they could have been annihilated, they focussed on God-given ***life*** *and refused to be tainted by the habits and possessions of the godless and the dead ... They separated themselves as far as they could from the behaviour of their enemies. They behaved differently from what was expected.*[9]

The grace of God that delivered the Jews from the hand of their enemies was reflected in the restraint the Jews showed in their defence. God's grace enables God's people to behave in a way that is different from the rest of the world. It empowers us to forgive and go on forgiving. It allows us to view ourselves as we really are: sinners, rescued from death by a merciful God. It prompts compassion and mercy in our response to those who hurt, offend or mistreat us. It frees us from the need to avenge wrong *ourselves* and releases us to trust *God* as our defence and righteous judge.

We see an even greater example of grace in Jesus' response to His enemies as He suffered on the cross and prayed, 'Father, forgive them, for they do not know what they are doing' (Lk. 23:34).

REFLECTION

Who do you need to show grace and forgiveness to? Pray that the Holy Spirit would enable you to do that.

DAY 27

READ Esther 9:18–32

The book of Esther starts and ends with a feast of celebration. The first is a celebration of a proud king's wealth and majesty. The final feast is a celebration of God's faithfulness and mercy to His people.

In chapter 3 we read that Haman cast a *pur*, that is a lot, to select the day and month on which the Jews would be destroyed (3:7). The plural of the word *pur* is *purim*. This became the name for the feast of celebration that the Jews would observe every year to remind them of their deliverance from Haman's plot.

Haman's *pur* fell on the thirteenth day of the twelfth month, the month of Adar. That was the day chosen for the destruction of God's people across the province. But the Jews were not destroyed on the thirteenth day of the month of Adar. They were saved as they defended themselves from their enemies. Then they were able to rest and enjoy a day of feasting and joy (vv. 17–18).

The Jews had great cause to celebrate Purim annually (vv. 20–21, 27–32). The day that would have marked their death and annihilation became a day of hope for future life. The day that would have been marked by mourning and sadness was now characterised by rejoicing and celebrating. God's people had been delivered from death by the hand of God, intervening in a hidden but nonetheless powerful and sovereign way. An appropriate response to their salvation was to celebrate with joy (v. 22).

We have been saved from death in a no less dramatic way than the Jews in Persia. When we were lost in our sin, heading hopelessly towards a dreadful and eternal punishment in hell, God intervened and provided a saviour, His son Jesus Christ. Because of Jesus' death and resurrection, we are eternally saved from destruction. We are free from the threat of death. It no longer hangs over us, clouding our days with despair and fear.

We have every reason to celebrate God's saving work in our lives. So we need to regularly spend time rejoicing in the gospel and praising God for His wonderful salvation. C.J. Mahaney writes,

Reminding ourselves of the gospel is the most important daily habit we can establish. If the gospel is the most vital news in the world, and if salvation by grace is the defining truth of our existence, we should create ways to immerse ourselves in these truths every day. No days off allowed.[10]

REFLECTION

How do you celebrate your salvation? Are you so weighed down with the cares and worries of life that you've forgotten to rejoice in all that God has done for you in Jesus? Pray for a renewed perspective.

DAY 28

READ Esther 10:1–3

At the end of the ten-year story of Esther, King Xerxes still ruled over the 127 provinces from India to Cush, and his power and might were still recognised throughout his vast empire.

Verse 1 tells us that Xerxes imposed a tribute throughout the empire. This was a tax increase imposed on all of the inhabitants of the kingdom. When a Persian monarch made a new tax arrangement they were said to 'lay a tribute on the land'. Since Xerxes had previously lost some of his territories during the war with Greece and had then lost thousands of lives when the Jews defended themselves against their attackers, it's not surprising that he would seek to increase his income in this way.

Mordecai also became incredibly powerful and respected across the empire. He is described in verse 2 as a man of 'greatness' and verse 3 gives us four reasons for that.

1 **Mordecai was 'second in rank to King Xerxes, pre-eminent among the Jews'.** Persia was a Gentile empire and the Jews living there did so only by permission of the government. That a Jew was made second in command to King Xerxes would have been surprising to both Jews and Gentiles.

2 **Mordecai was 'held in high esteem by his many fellow Jews'.** The Jews of Persia knew of Mordecai's words and actions on their behalf and they honoured him. Unlike Xerxes, Mordecai didn't govern through fear and control. He wasn't greedy or self-serving. He didn't seek to honour himself or Esther but God alone. So the Jews respected Mordecai and thought highly of him.

3 **Mordecai 'worked for the good of his people'.** Mordecai wasn't primarily concerned with his own good or that of his family. He cared about all of God's people, across all 127 provinces of the empire, and he worked hard to bring about peace and protection for them.

4 **Mordecai 'spoke up for the welfare of all the Jews'.** In some translations this sentence reads, 'spoke peace to all his people'. Chapter 9 verse 30 tells us that Mordecai sent 'words of goodwill and assurance' to the Jews across the province. Mordecai spoke a message of hope and security to the Jews. Undoubtedly his words of assurance and peace point forward to Jesus, the promised Prince of Peace.

Mordecai failed to receive an immediate reward for saving Xerxes' life at the end of Esther 2. He became the object of Haman's hatred and persecution in chapters 3 and 5. But at the end of the book Mordecai is honoured, not just by Xerxes but by his fellow Jews throughout the kingdom.

REFLECTION

Read 2 Thessalonians 1:6–7. Pray for patience in trials and confidence in God's justice.

DAY 29 **READ** Esther 2:5–9, 17; 4:12–16; 8:1–8

The book of Esther might be summarised by some readers as a Cinderella story: a rags-to-riches tale in which the wise and dignified heroine saves the day and lives happily ever after in the palace. But the story of Esther isn't a Cinderella story; it's a saviour story.

Esther was in many ways a heroine. She demonstrated the kind of godly character that we, as followers of Jesus, want to cultivate in our own lives. Her commitment to God and His purposes was evident. She was available as God's chosen instrument, ready to be used by Him for the salvation of His people.

Likewise, Mordecai was in many ways a hero. His wisdom, strength and humility shine through the pages of the story and it was his trust in God's promises and his uncompromising faith that resulted in Esther's actions. It is fitting that the book of Esther ends with a tribute to him.

But the real hero of the story, the real saviour, is neither Esther nor Mordecai but God Himself. His name is not written in the pages of this book. But in every scene His hand is at work, directing, preparing and ordering people and events with invisible providence so that His purposes would be accomplished. He is 'silent but sovereign'.

Esther drifts in and out of the recorded scenes of this ten-year story. But God is active in every scene. He is silent but working; invisible but ever-present. Matthew Henry wrote about the book of Esther, 'Though the name of God be not in it, the finger of God is directing many minute events for the bringing about of his people's deliverance.'[11]

Like Esther, we live as God's people in an ungodly society. Our world is governed by rulers who have little regard for God's word and His desires for the world He created. God's people around the world have always known rejection and persecution, and increasingly in the West Christians are marginalised and treated with less respect and favour than others in society.

Just as God was active in every scene in the book of Esther, He is active in every scene of our lives. He is deeply concerned for His church. He is deeply concerned for the honour of His name. He will not allow anyone, however powerful, to thwart even one of His plans for His children. He is not defeated or discouraged when sinful men prevail, when laws are passed that contradict His word or when it seems that Satan has the upper hand. He refuses to be distracted from His work of redeeming a people for Himself.

REFLECTION

How has the book of Esther encouraged you to trust in God's sovereignty, especially when His activity is hidden?

DAY 30 READ Esther 1:1–8; 2:19–23; 10:1–2

Ten years after the story of Esther finishes, Great King Xerxes was the subject of another assassination attempt, but this one was successful. Xerxes was killed by Artabanus, the commander of the royal bodyguard, and his son Artexerxes succeeded him as king. Nothing more is said about Esther or Mordecai or events in Susa. Eventually the entire empire collapsed under the rule of Greece.

But God is still on His throne today and His kingdom is an eternal kingdom. It's a kingdom that is still growing, as in surprising and unexpected ways He is working to bring people from all around the world to know Him. It's a kingdom that will never collapse because when Jesus rose from the dead, He defeated sin and Satan completely and secured our salvation for eternity.

While we live in this world, we are still affected by and often hurt by the consequences of the fall and by sinful behaviour – our own and that of others. But when we reach heaven, our future home, we will see Jesus reigning in majesty and glory. There will be no more suffering, brokenness, tears, arguments or tragedies. Jesus will be the centre of our attention. He will radiate light and beauty, and we will spend eternity in His presence, praising and glorifying Him as we finally see Him as He is.

Although He's not mentioned in the book of Esther, it should be Jesus who captures our hearts as we see how the story points to Him as our perfect and eternal saviour. The achievements of Esther and Mordecai point ahead to the greater achievements that Jesus' death and resurrection declare.

- Esther and Mordecai were used by God to save people from one nation at one time in history. But Jesus saves people from every nation throughout every generation of history.
- Esther and Mordecai saved people from a premature and unjust death. But Jesus saves people from a fully deserved and eternal death.
- Esther and Mordecai brought peace, for a time, between God's people and King Xerxes. But Jesus brings peace between God's people and God Himself for eternity.

Esther and Mordecai were great examples of godly people, who trusted God and who shone brightly for Him in a dark and ungodly world. But Jesus is our eternal hope of salvation and joy.

REFLECTION

How does the book of Esther encourage you to love Jesus more? How does it encourage you to look forward to eternity in heaven?

REFERENCES

1 Chapman, Mary Beth, *Choosing to SEE: A Journey of Struggle and Hope* (Revell, a division of Baker Publishing Group, 2011).

2 Keil, C.F., *Commentary on the Old Testament in Ten Volumes*, vol. III (William B. Eerdmans Publishing Company, 1966).

3 Roseveare, Dr Helen, *Give Me This Mountain* (Christian Focus Publications, 2006).

4 Piper, John, *Don't Waste Your Life* (IVP, 2005).

5 Mahaney, C.J., *Humility: True Greatness* (Multnomah Press, 2005).

6 Yancey, Philip, *Disappointment with God* (Zondervan, 1988).

7 Eareckson-Tada, Joni, *Heaven: Your Real Home* (Zondervan, 1997).

8 St Augustine, *Handbook on Faith, Hope and Love* (Christian Classics Ethereal Library, 2009).

9 McNabb, Jane, *Daylight at Midnight* (Authentic Media, 2007).

10 Mahaney, C.J., *Living the Cross Centered Life* (Multnomah Press, 2006).

11 Matthew Henry, *Commentary on the Whole Bible* (Zondervan, 1960).

MORE IN THIS SERIES

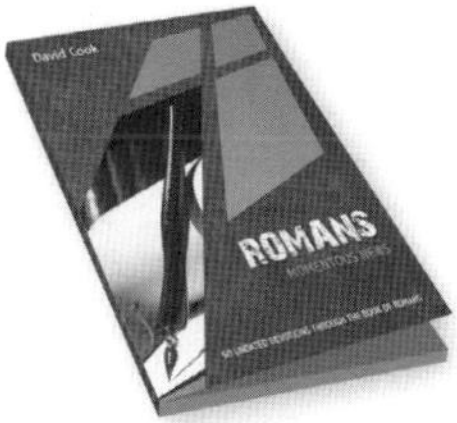

ROMANS
Momentous News
By David Cook
ISBN: 978-1-906173-24-1

MARK
The Suffering Servant
By Jeremy McQuoid
ISBN: 978-1-906173-55-5

DANIEL
Far From Home
By Justin Mote
ISBN: 978-1-906173-68-5

1 THESSALONIANS
Living for Jesus
By Julia Marsden
ISBN: 978-1-906173-67-8

PHILIPPIANS
Press towards the Goal
By Kay Mumford
ISBN: 978-1-909611-31-3

GALATIANS
The Life I Now Live
By Peter Mead
ISBN: 978-1-910587-09-6

ACTS
To the Ends of the Earth
By David Cook
ISBN: 978-1-909611-02-3

EZEKIEL
For His Glory
By Peter Lau
ISBN: 978-1-909611-83-2

JOHN
Never Thirst Again
By David Cook
ISBN: 978-1-909611-30-6

10 Publishing
a division of 10ofthose.com

To place an order call: **0844 879 3243** email: **sales@10ofthose.com**
or order online: **www.10ofthose.com**

Carolyn Lacey
ESTHER
SILENT BUT SOVEREIGN
30 UNDATED DEVOTIONS THROUGH THE BOOK OF ESTHER